The Ghosts of
TOTNES

Bob Mann

GW00500228

OBELISK PUBLICATIONS

Also by the Author:
Boat Trip Down the Dart
Other Titles in This Series
Ghosts of Exeter, Sally & Chips Barber
Ghosts of Torbay, Deryck Seymour
Ghosts of Berry Pomeroy Castle, Deryck Seymour
Ghosts of Brixham, Graham Wyley
Tales of the Unexplained in Devon, Judy Chard
Haunted Happenings in Devon, Judy Chard
Tales of the Teign, Chips Barber & Judy Chard
Dark & Dastardly Dartmoor, Sally & Chips Barber
Weird & Wonderful Dartmoor, Sally & Chips Barber
Ghastly and Ghostly Devon, Sally & Chips Barber

Other Obelisk Publications About This Area
Totnes Collection, Bill Bennett
Great Little Totnes Book, Chips Barber & Bill Bennett
Under Sail Thr South Devon & Dartmoor, R. B. Cattell
Diary of a Devonshire Walker, Chips Barber
Diary of a Dartmoor Walker, Chips Barber
Great Little Dartmoor Book, Chips Barber
Made in Devon, Chips Barber & David FitzGerald
Burgh Island & Bigbury Bay, Chips Barber & Judy Chard
Dartmoor in Colour, Chips Barber
Torbay in Colour, Chips Barber
The South Hams, Chips Barber
Walks in the South Hams, Brian Carter
Around and About Salcombe, Chips Barber
Walking with a Tired Terrier In and Around Torbay, Brian Carter
Ten Family Walks on Dartmoor, Sally & Chips Barber

If you would like further details of currently available titles, please send an s.a.e. to the address below or telephone (0392) 468556.

This little book is dedicated to Samantha Benedikte, writer, healer and Buddhist.

ACKNOWLEDGEMENTS
I would like to thank all those people, named and anonymous, who supplied me with the stories in this book. Thanks also to Maya Hussell, Chips and Sally Barber, Ellen Mann, Sam Richards, Bill Bennett MBE of the Totnes Museum and Museum Study Centre, and Trevor Drew, editor of the *Totnes Times* for permission to recycle some of the material, though not the ghosts themselves, which appeared in my 'Innside Stories' and 'Mann About Town' columns.

PLATE ACKNOWLEDGEMENTS
Jane Reynolds for cover and all drawings apart from page 13
Chips Barber supplied pictures on pages 5, 8, 14, 22 and 24
Sally Barber for map on page 17

First published in 1993 by
Obelisk Publications, 2 Church Hill, Pinhoe, Exeter, Devon
Designed by Chips and Sally Barber
Typeset by Sally Barber
Printed in Great Britain
by Maslands Limited, Tiverton, Devon.

INTRODUCTION

Totnes is an ancient market town on the River Dart in South Devon, and is well-known for many things: its beautiful and historic buildings, its ideal setting as a holiday centre between Torbay and Dartmoor, its 'Elizabethan' Tuesdays in the summer and, more recently, its reputation as a focus for all kinds of 'New Age' therapies and lifestyles. It is a diverse and creative community that is yet of manageable size, a small town that has something of the cultural ambience of a small city.

However, it is not particularly known for its ghosts! Totnes is hardly ever mentioned in collections of Devon ghost stories, and when I first began researching for this book I was not sure if I would find enough material, as I only knew about a couple of hauntings in the town and a few vague memories of others. But after asking around, I discovered that Totnes has at least its fair share of supernatural phenomena, including a surprising number of haunted pubs. One or two of the ghosts seem to be purely traditional, but others are active today, and if you are in the right place at the right time you could well experience one of them (though please respect people's privacy). They range from uncanny feelings and strange atmospheres to full-blown apparitions and even some mild poltergeist activity.

At first sight it may seem odd that Totnes, being so old a town, has not many more traditional ghost stories and legends. Founded early in the tenth century by the Saxon kingdom of Wessex as a fortified borough against the Danes, it has nearly eleven centuries of life behind it, and should be crawling with shades and spectres from the past, yet there are comparatively few stories that have been handed down for any length of time. One reason for this may lie in the social history of the town. For at least 300 years Totnes has been quite a genteel, cultivated place in which to settle, and the railway arrived in 1847, linking it directly to London and the rest of the country. Consequently, Totnes has been less isolated, physically and culturally, than so many communities in Devon, and the timeless, archaic folk-life in which traditional lore flourishes has been less apparent. Even that most ubiquitous character in folklore, the Devil, has not been a frequent visitor, although some sources say that the Devil's Hoofprints, the mysterious tracks that appeared all over South and East Devon one winter morning in 1855, were seen as far west as Totnes (the whole story can be found in another book in this series, *The Ghosts of Exeter* by Sally and Chips Barber).

On the other hand, it could be that Totnes once had as much traditional material as anywhere, but it just wasn't ever 'collected'. When, in the nineteenth century, enthusiastic vicars and antiquaries were avidly researching 'peasant' superstitions, folktales and songs, no one thought to interview the older inhabitants of Totnes, and so the local stories were forgotten. Thus, while the ghost of Weaver Knowles at Dean Prior, near Buckfastleigh, was recorded and has been written about in book after book ever since, the similar story of Mayor Chadder in Totnes only survived in the private papers of one family, and was therefore unknown – until now (see page 21).

As to the reality of ghosts: my own attitude is one of cautious open-mindedness. I have never, to my knowledge, seen (or heard) an apparition, but I am sensitive to atmospheres and occasionally pick up feelings and impressions about a place. I am attracted to the theory that some ghosts, at least, may be a kind of place-memory, recorded onto the atmosphere by strong emotion under certain weather conditions (often warm and wet), in a way that could be analogous to holograms. I personally find it difficult to accept the idea of disembodied spirits or unseen entities floating around; to me, the spiritual and physical aspects of life are inseparable, and I cannot see how you can have one manifesting without the other, but I have no wish to be dogmatic about this. Poltergeists, it is generally agreed, take their energy from living persons for their tiresome activities. In the end, no one yet knows what ghosts 'really' are or how they work, and many people who have written about the supernatural have noted, with amusement or despair according to temperament, that there is always just a little too much evidence to be dismissed completely, but never quite enough to wholly convince the sceptic. Whatever the truth may be, in this book I am content just to relay the stories for your entertainment, without getting bogged down in theory. I am sure of the honesty and integrity of all my informants, and though I have to confess that one of the ghosts is decidedly tongue-in-cheek, even it is not totally fictitious!

Here, then, for the first time ever, is a publication devoted to the ghosts of Totnes and its immediate environment. We start at the top of the town and make our way, in a meandering fashion, down to the river and across to Bridgetown, before visiting the nearby mansions of Bowden and Dartington and then walking through some of the surrounding lanes. The stories feature many well-known people and familiar buildings, and it gives me great pleasure to present this study of a hitherto neglected aspect of my home town. If you know of stories I have not included, or have experiences connected with any I have, please let me know of them.

Bay Horse Inn, Cistern Street

This pleasant old slate-hung town pub faces the area where, for centuries, the sheep market took place, and this end of Totnes still has the atmosphere of an old-fashioned Devon market town. The inn itself is possibly five hundred years old, and always gives me a satisfying sense of the quiet continuity of Totnes life over the centuries. It is reputed to be haunted by the ghost of a little old man in a red coat.

A few years ago the Bay Horse was kept by the late Harold Hall, a retired policeman. Late one night a friend was sitting in the lounge after the other customers had gone, talking to Harold behind the bar. The lights in the public bar, behind the landlord, were still on, though there was nobody in the room. The friend then noticed a figure in red walking through the public bar towards the end of the room, and said to Harold, "There's still someone in the bar." Harold turned around on his stool, looked, and said, "There's nobody in there." "Yes there is," insisted the customer, "A man in red." The landlord summoned his wife, who had been out of earshot, and asked her if she had seen anyone. "Was he wearing red?" she asked. "That's our ghost!"

As far as I know, nothing ghostly has been seen here since, and the current licensees have not seen or heard anything out of the ordinary.

Kingsbridge Inn, Leechwell Street

This lovely old inn has long been one of my favourite places in Totnes, full of charm, character, cosy corners, good food and well-kept ale. It is the oldest inn in Totnes, but no one knows exactly how old, its origins being lost in the mists of the past. Parts of the building are fourteenth century, though most of what is here today is probably

seventeenth century. There is no doubt, however, that there has been an inn here for a very long time.

I have always known the Kingsbridge to be haunted; in fact for ages I thought it was about the only place in the town that was. It is still one of the most haunted buildings in Totnes, and people who have known it for over fifty years can remember it as always being the scene of strange happenings and unexplained apparitions.

The most persistent ghost is that of a woman, believed to have been an unfortunate seventeenth century barmaid called Mary Brown. The story is that she was seduced, and later murdered, by the landlord, and buried in the walls of the building. This story, however, does not appear to be very old, and its truth (or lack of it) makes no difference to the reality of the ghost itself. If you are at all sensitive to psychic phenomena you could well experience something at the Kingsbridge, but it helps if you happen to be female! The ghost usually only likes to show herself to women, perhaps, if the story is true, because of her treatment by a man.

The young daughter of the family who kept the inn during the 1970s came face to face with the woman at the top of the stairs, and took several days to recover from the shock. During the occupancy of the next owners the ghost was particularly active, and it seems to have been then that the theory of the murdered barmaid was developed. A report in the *Morning Advertiser*, the newspaper of the licensed trade, for July 1st 1980, states that the figure of a tall, dark, quiet woman had often been seen by various people, standing at the bar and gliding through to the kitchen, where the chef and waiting staff had grown quite used to seeing her. The landlady was quoted as saying, "The first time I saw her was just after we moved in some eighteen months ago. I looked through a window and saw a figure in the corner of the bar. It was a tall woman but then she suddenly vanished. When I first came to see the property I didn't know anything about a ghost but I felt freezing cold, and at times even now I feel as if someone is watching me." The owners' dog was also apparently aware of something unseen, and would bark at empty tables, as do the dogs who live at the pub today.

In October 1989 the Kingsbridge was bought by Jane and Martyn Canevali and Jane's parents, Rosemary and Paul Triggs. They have taken a great interest in the hauntings, and Jane and Rosemary have both seen the woman, who always wears her hair in a bun. One evening a reflection was seen in the glass door, and there was a sudden drop in temperature, which was confirmed by two other ladies who were present. Later in the evening they realised that the reflection could not have been of anyone who was there, because no one had her hair in a bun like the image did!

Rosemary saw the ghost one lunchtime whilst serving customers. She looked up and was suddenly aware of "a misty outline of a lady facing the blackboard next to the stairs. When I looked up again she was gone." On another occasion, Rosemary was sleeping at the inn when she felt intense cold, which she recognised as being unnatural. Impatiently she said, "That's enough, now go away" and the temperature returned to normal.

Martyn came close to experiencing the ghost one autumn morning shortly after he had opened the pub. There were about a dozen people there, when two ladies arrived who wanted to sit near one of the fires. The table next to the fire in the bar was occupied, so they looked into the pump room, exclaiming in disappointment that there was already someone, a woman, sitting by that fire as well. Martyn knew he had not served an unaccompanied woman that morning, so he "shot into the pump room, to be confronted by an area devoid of customers, never mind a lady on her own." Could the visitors have seen Mary Brown?

The pump room, so-called because it contains an old water pump connected to the nearby Leechwells (of which more in a minute), is a lovely, comfortable space which you never want to leave, the walls seeming to be several feet thick, though it was actually once an uncovered courtyard. A medium once visited the inn for the first time, and was seen to take a step back from the pump in alarm. She advised that there should always be a bright light shining on it, which there has been ever since, and the area is attractively decorated with plants and pebbles.

A previous landlord of the inn, who took no interest in ghosts, once told me that the only haunting he knew of was connected with this room. He understood that there was once a very old carved chair kept in there, which had belonged to a long-dead elderly lady who had once been the landlady. So attached to it was she that she was sometimes seen sitting in it after her death. Unfortunately a later owner of the pub took the chair with him when he left.

Sightings of the lady and other inexplicable occurrences continue unabated at the Kingsbridge Inn, appropriately enough for such an old and atmospheric place.

A Walk with a Grey Lady

Grey Ladies are probably the most common form of traditional ghost in England, gentle shades whose sightings have been recorded since the sixteenth century. They possibly began as folk-memories of the nuns who cared for the sick during the Middle Ages, and are often associated with old hospitals, but crop up everywhere, whether there was ever an establishment of nuns there or not.

There are memories of a Grey Lady being seen in several parts of Totnes and over in Bridgetown; or perhaps there are several different Grey Ladies! Assuming she is the same one, she has quite a perambulation of the town. Her walk, as I heard about it a few years ago, seems to be as follows.

She begins at the ancient Leechwell, which is reached by a short path immediately outside the Kingsbridge Inn on the right. The three troughs of the well are called 'Snake', 'Toad' and 'Long Crippler' and their waters were used respectively for the treatment of snake bite, skin disease and blindness. It is common for ancient healing wells to be associated with ghostly ladies, usually in white, and obviously descended from pre-Christian nature spirits. Possibly our Lady contains a dim memory of this. From the well the delightful Leechwell Lane, a place of high walls covered with flowers and crack plants, overarching trees and distant glimpses of countryside, takes you across to the town. The lane is known locally as 'Leper's Walk', the idea being that patients from the medieval leper hospital of St Mary Magdalen would, after bathing at the well, take this enclosed route to the church. This is totally erroneous, as the whole point of the hospital was to keep them away from the town. No matter – the lane has a beautifully quiet, secluded ambience to it, and this is somehow not spoiled by the road which has been knocked through it! Surprisingly, I have never heard of anyone seeing or otherwise experiencing a ghost here, as of all places in Totnes it seems the most suitable for one. However, our Grey Lady, ancient water nymph by way of nun, walks not towards the town, but turns up from the well into Maudlin Road, going left down the hill. The hospital was somewhere along here, but all trace of it has long since vanished.

Our shadowy guide goes to the end of the road and turns left down Moat Hill to Warland, where she has definitely been sighted. Someone who lives here tells me that she was once informed that opposite her house was a nuns' graveyard, but this is difficult to believe, as the land was marsh until a couple of centuries ago, and there was never any house of nuns in Totnes. There was a medieval chapel at Warland dedicated to St Katherine, but this was served by Friars, not nuns.

Apparently the lady now crosses the river to Bridgetown where she was seen, not too many years ago, in a garden just below the Cottage Hospital, appropriately for such an

apparition, though the hospital only dates from 1901. The place where she was seen is now part of the Kings Orchard estate.

Unfortunately there is no historical evidence that there were ever nuns at the leper hospital, the chapel there being served by Benedictine monks from Totnes Priory. However, whatever her origins, the Grey Lady has been seen at places along the route we have just taken, if not very recently.

Cherry Cross and Dart Villas

Just above where the Grey Lady turns down Moat Hill is Cherry Cross, possibly, with St Peter's Quay down by the river, the earliest settlement of Totnes. The cross itself is a restored one of the Middle Ages, standing by the roadside with a little semi-circular wall behind it. It is now backed by comfortable bungalows, but when I was a child it was almost set into a high Devon hedgebank. The story I heard then was that, if you walked backwards round the cross three times, you would see the Devil. Another version, that I was told only recently, is that a face appears in the little window of the old coach-house just up the hill, at the entrance to Dart Villas. I never tried it, but someone who did saw a shadowy figure hovering nearby, and promptly ran as fast as possible down the hill! The area today is one of pleasant homes with beautiful views out over the town and countryside, but some people feel uncomfortable in the vicinity of the cross and say that the energy there is, if not negative, decidedly strange.

Dart Villas, just above the cross, are four large, spacious houses, clearly visible for miles. Some years ago a black dog lived at one of them, and he would regularly go and visit his neighbours next door. So fond of doing this did he become, in fact, that he was observed to go on doing it after he had died! I am sure it is only an interesting coincidence that ghostly black dogs are so often associated with the area of an ancient crossroads, but it shows that, even in sophisticated Totnes, old beliefs, superstitions and archetypal material are only just beneath the surface.

Plymouth Road

Returning to the top of the main street in the town, just down from the Bay Horse Inn and off to the left is Plymouth Road. The tall, attractive houses on the left were built in the 1840s by the great Brunel for the engineers and craftsmen involved in the construction of his ingenious but impractical Atmospheric Railway between Newton Abbot and Totnes (the navvies, of course, stayed in rather less salubrious accommodation some way out of town). Each house is slightly different, being designed, with typical nineteenth century thoroughness, for the occupation of the man inhabiting it: one was for the smith, having a separate entrance to the forge; the one that concerns us now contained the drawing-office. In the days when the houses were put up there were no buildings opposite, and the occupants, each morning, had an uninterrupted view up the valley of the railway line's progress.

At the end of 1986 Steve and Heather, a Totnes couple long known to me, moved into one of the houses with their two young sons. They had no odd feelings about the place at the time but, by a strange quirk of fate, on the very day they signed the contract the previous owner, an elderly man who had lived in the house for about forty years, passed away in an old people's home. Heather, who told me about their experiences, thinks it must be he who began making his presence known shortly after.

First to encounter him was their eldest son Liam, then aged two. He began waking up in the night and seeing an old man in the room with him. The man looked solid enough, but said nothing, which upset Liam as he

likes people to talk to him. Soon afterwards Heather, getting up in the night, found the man standing outside the bathroom. He was dressed in ordinary clothes and looked perfectly life-like. Apart from understandable surprise, she got no bad feeling from his presence. Steve was completely sceptical, but not long after this a young woman who was staying with them and sleeping in the attic woke to see before her a woman, brushing her hair, watched by the old man. The next night Steve and Heather held a party, and several guests, visiting the bathroom, wondered whose grandfather the old man on the stairs was! The girl who had slept in the attic recognised him. On the following night another woman sleeping there was almost pulled out of bed by some unknown force.

After this nothing happened for a while, except that one night Heather found the old man in his usual place outside the bathroom. Then there was a gap of about ten months before the phenomena resumed.

She has noticed a sort of pattern to the occurrences. First the man would be seen, by herself or someone else. The appearances became more frequent and then something dramatic would happen, like the friend being pulled out of bed. It is as if energy was being built up towards some physical demonstration. Whenever the couple started working on another room in the house, the ghost began to remind them of his existence. In the most recent phase, objects started to move and noises were heard when there was nobody there to cause the disturbances. Steve, ever sceptical, thought it might be cats or wind, but neither explanation was possible. Several people staying in the house heard sounds and saw movements.

Nothing has happened since November 1990, and although Heather told me that the man had a tendency to appear after she talked about him, he has not done so since my investigation early in 1991. However she still feels that there is an unseen person with them in the house, and that he is probably the man who lived there for so long before them, who simply wants to retain his connection with it.

Queen's Terrace

Down near the railway station, where Castle Street comes out to the main road, is this row of solid red-brick Victorian houses. Before they were built, all the land on this side of Totnes was quite marshy, and there is a belief that patients from the leper hospital were buried hereabouts, though this seems unlikely as the hospital was so far away and there would have been plenty of space nearer to it for such a purpose. Anyway, a family moved into one of the houses a few years ago, and the mother, who is the only one of them to have experienced anything supernatural in it tells me that she immediately felt that there was some kind of 'presence' there, especially on the landing. One night she became aware that something was following her and, looking round, she saw the face – and only the face! – of a young man who, she says "looked as if he was in his early 30s, with high blood pressure and a mischievous expression." Understandably, she went cold and felt the hair on the back of her head rise up in fear. After this she always kept the landing light on, and did not see the face again, but continued to feel his presence. Shortly after this her sister-in-law was staying with them, and she also felt strongly that there was someone there. She recommended telling whoever it was to go away, which was done, in no uncertain terms. This seemed to work, as nothing more was felt for several years.

Then, at the beginning of 1991, the mother again had an encounter with the young man's ghost, but not, this time, with his face. Feeling something push her on the stairs she looked down to see a man's torso wearing a rough-looking brown jacket, but with no head or lower body! Fortunately, there have been no manifestations since then.

At another house in the same terrace the ghost of an old man, a former resident, has been seen sitting outside the back door of what was once his home.

Swansfoot, South Street

Hauntings by swans are, as far as I know, extremely rare, but the ghost of a one-footed swan must be unique! Yet such is the one associated with a small house at the top end of South Street, on the lower side of the wall just after it divides. The house, dating from about 1750, is now called 'Swansfoot' in honour of the story, which begins when the place was bought, in rather a run-down condition, by Ross McCulloch, at the beginning of 1990. While working on the house, Ross and the builders found a small cavity in a partition on the front wall, and inside it was the desiccated foot of a swan. There was nothing else there, no explanation for such a bizarre relic, and local experts on history and folklore were unable to offer any ideas as to what it was doing there. After about a week, though, Ross began to notice odd occurrences, and one night, during a full moon, he distinctly heard a sound like the beating of wings and the noise of a large bird scrabbling about on the roof.

Shortly after this I happened to be organising an exhibition with a difference on the history and culture of Devon, in which people were invited to provide objects or artifacts which they felt summed up, or said something essential about, the county and its character. Amongst the many diverse exhibits I received was the foot, which Ross had beautifully mounted and framed, with a little card explaining where it had come from. It would be difficult to say whether or not it was the strangest of the objects which purported to epitomise England's loveliest county, but it certainly had an impact on most of the people who saw it, especially the young women, who didn't like it at all. Ross confessed to having misgivings about it leaving the house, even for two nights, but at the end of the weekend it was returned safely, no harm having come to it or anything else. In fact it was good from the point of view of finding out more, because a few of the older Totnes people who saw the foot remembered stories of a ghostly swan that was said to fly up from the river at nightfall, circling slowly and landing, rather awkwardly, on the roof of the house! Apparently Ross's house was once inhabited by a poacher, and perhaps the story commemorates the theft, long ago, of one of the royal birds – or maybe only its foot? Is the other one also hidden in the walls? Whatever the truth of the matter, the foot remains in the house, still in its frame, and Ross feels that its influence is benign, though he is careful to treat it with respect.

Ramparts Walk and The Guildhall

Probably the most attractive part of old Totnes is Ramparts Walk, which runs behind St Mary's Church, past the Guildhall, and follows the original line of the town wall to the East Gate. A high, narrow, cobbled pathway, bright with flowers and redolent of the town's generally quiet life through the centuries, it is just the kind of romantic area where you would expect a ghost to be found, gliding along in the moonlight next to the churchyard, and several people who live nearby claim to have seen one, a lady in Elizabethan dress, doing just that!

Then there is the Guildhall itself. This marvellous building is like a distillation of Totnes' history and tradition. It has been the centre of the town's civic life since 1553, but the lower chamber was originally the refectory of the Benedictine Priory founded by Judhael, Norman overlord of Totnes, in 1088. With its long list of mayors going back to 1359, its paintings and records of eminent  Totnesians, odd objects like the bullring and mantrap and its prison cells, the Guildhall is a fascinating place where the sensitive visitor can absorb the essence of the past. But it is very much a working building as well, being the headquarters and meeting place of the Town Council, and it is regularly used by local organisations for their AGMs and other business.

If devotion to a building by someone leads to it being haunted by them, then in the future the Guildhall is going to be haunted by Paul Honeywill, its tireless custodian! Paul, who is also a well-known local artist and illustrator, spends much of his life here, and seems to know all there is to be known about it. He tells me that, though no one has yet reported actually seeing a ghost, many visitors seem to freeze at the top of the staircase leading to the council chamber, and one man said that the spot is definitely haunted. Paul himself often feels that things are going on just outside his range of vision; he is aware, out of the corner of his eye, of figures moving about. Maybe they are past mayors and burghers of Totnes, returning to the place where they conducted the town's affairs, or perhaps those soldiers of Cromwell who were billeted here, some of whom died here of the plague, which they brought to Totnes. Or maybe they are the centuries-old shades of the silent monks who were here before anyone. When Paul has been in the lower chamber at the end of the day, counting up the money, he has sometimes been

In the Stocks, at Totnes Old Guild Hall.

aware of being watched. If one considers the life that the Guildhall has seen over the centuries, it is maybe not surprising that in this seemingly 'timeless' building, some of the energy of previous times is still around!

1 Ramparts Walk

One of the more dramatic events to happen in Totnes in recent years was the great fire of September 4th 1990, which made national headlines. The East Gate arch and several properties were gutted, and firemen from all over Devon worked all night to save the historic heart of the town from being completely lost. Among the buildings destroyed was 1 Ramparts Walk, dating from the fourteenth century, which, like the others, has now been rebuilt. Before the fire the flat at number 1 was the home of Mrs Audrey Bulley, who lived there with her late husband Harry. Mrs Bulley had been in the flat for four years when, having occasion to get up at around 3 a.m. one morning, she entered the passage and saw the apparition of a man in Elizabethan costume leaning against the door of the spare room. It being the time of night it was, she knew he could not be one of the Totnes Elizabethans who dress up on Tuesdays during the summer for the benefit of tourists! Rigid with fear, she had time to take in his appearance. He wore, she says, "the usual bulging pants with slits of white over black velvet, a green velvet coat buttoned to the waist, long stockings with silver-buckled shoes and a velvet cap with the longest feather I have ever seen, stretching from the front of the cap to below his waist." When the man saw her frightened face and heard her gasps, he gave her a broad and wicked grin!

14

About three weeks later she saw him again, this time blocking her bedroom doorway. Feeling more sure of herself, Mrs Bulley just said, "Oh, you again!" and walked through him! This seems to have put him off appearing, but he continued to make his presence felt.

Both Mrs Bulley and Harry were aware of the man: each time they walked along the passage they felt him, unseen, coming the other way, and sometimes he would push them roughly. On one occasion he pushed Harry so hard that he almost fell into the kitchen, and only avoided a nasty bump on the head by grabbing the sink. Mrs Bulley told me she 'really blew her top' at this, and after that they only received the odd nudges until one day when Mrs Bulley and Harry's daughter, Pam, were standing each side of the kitchen doorway, talking to Harry inside the kitchen. The ghost pushed rudely against Pam and threw her stepmother forward. They had hoped to keep all knowledge of their ghost from Pam, but of course now she had to be told. The man's other irritating habit was to remove objects, although he later gave them back, all except the four aces from a pack of cards, which were never seen again. This continued up until a week before the fire.

A former occupant of 1A Ramparts Walk also saw the tiresome Elizabethan, no less than six times, and came to Mrs Bulley convinced she was going out of her mind. Their descriptions of the man were exactly the same. This lady now lives in Paignton.

After Mr Bulley's death, his widow moved to the smaller bedroom. In the early hours of one morning she awoke and felt a presence near her. Thinking it must be a burglar, and stiff with fear, she opened her eyes slowly, only to see another ghost hovering there, this time of a lady. She was dressed in a more modern style to that of the Elizabethan, wearing "a dark frock with a V-neck collar of white. She had a pointed chin and beautiful wavy hair of a shining white colour." The apparition seemed to become aware of the fact that Mrs Bulley was awake and started to leave – in rather a startling manner. The man had disappeared quietly and all at once; the lady went in two halves, each one with a distinct 'bleeping' sound! This experience of a ghost making a noise when it vanishes has often been reported, but no explanation seems to exist. It suggests that we are dealing with real energy, that could perhaps be measured in some way.

Mrs Bulley told her landlord about her experiences. Mr Courtney Blake is a respected local businessman and a former mayor of Totnes, as down-to-earth a person as you could meet. He was not surprised to hear about the hauntings in his property, as the lady has been seen by at least three tenants over the years. He is himself sceptical of supernatural phenomena, but respects the beliefs of the witnesses, knowing them all to be people of integrity and sense. From the description of the female ghost he suggests that she could be a former tenant of his aunt's, a maiden lady from Dartington called Miss Barnes. I have been unable to find out who was living at the address during the Elizabethan period.

It will be interesting to find out whether the ghosts reappear now the house has been rebuilt.

Priory Gatehouse, 65 Fore Street

The playful 'spirit' of a little girl, possibly over four hundred years old, could still be making herself felt in this interesting and well-preserved building, which stands on its own just opposite the Museum. The house, built in around 1540 by another of the many prosperous Tudor merchants of Totnes, is on the site of the former gatehouse to the medieval Priory, dissolved just a few years before, and it may incorporate some of the earlier building. An inscription on the wall reads 'Priory Gatehouse of St Mary founded 1188 AD', but whoever wrote the inscription was a century out, as it was actually AD1088.

For the last few years the ground floor of the house has been a shoe shop, Steppin Stones, run by Mrs Margaret Stone, who chairs the Totnes Business Guild and is a fellow member of mine on the Town Council. Margaret has encountered ghosts before, and told me that as soon as she walked into the place she knew it was haunted. She and her staff have constantly been aware of something 'strange' in the atmosphere, and have experienced sudden inexplicable drops in temperature, a very common element in hauntings. In fact, as we talked in the shop one mild autumn afternoon, three of us clearly felt an unexpected coldness coming and going, completely unrelated to the weather outside, and this happens whenever Margaret talks about her haunting. I have felt sudden blasts of air whilst talking to her on many occasions since!

It was when she started selling children's shoes that more dramatic things started happening. She would come in to work in the morning and find shoe boxes all over the floor –

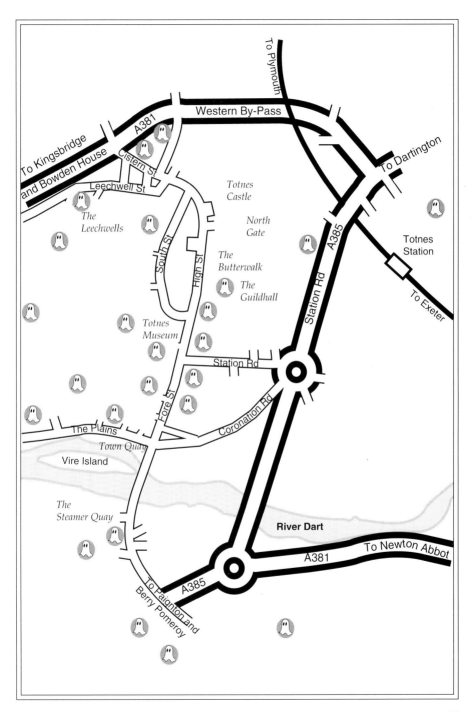

To Plymouth

Western By-Pass

A381

To Kingsbridge
and Bowden House

Cistern St

Leechwell St

*The
Leechwells*

South St

High St

*Totnes
Castle*

*North
Gate*

*The
Butterwalk*

*The
Guildhall*

To Dartington

Station Rd

A385

Totnes
Station

To Exeter

*Totnes
Museum*

Station Rd

Fore St

The Plains

Coronation Rd

Town Quay

Vire Island

*The
Steamer Quay*

River Dart

A381

To Newton Abbot

A385

To Paignton and
Berry Pomeroy

17

always children's shoes – and things generally moved about. There is no system to the disturbances; things may be thrown around at night or simply moved when someone's back is turned. Although no one has actually seen an apparition, everybody at the shop feels that the responsible entity is a little girl, mischievous rather than harmful and when something gets lost or moved they say "Naughty girl!" The haunting continues to this day. I was recently walking up the town one evening to a council meeting, and as I passed the shop I idly wondered whether the shoes had been thrown around lately, as all looked tidy enough in there. Five minutes later Margaret arrived at the meeting and told me that on her way up she had gone in and found shoes thrown everywhere.

Above the shoe shop, Simon Hocken has been running an independent dental practice since the end of 1990. While he was preparing the surgery and waiting area, working alone in the evenings, he frequently had the feeling that "someone had just left." There would be sudden changes of temperature, subtle drops or changes of light, little indications that there was another presence in the place. This feeling was especially strong around the stairwell, which is directly above Margaret's store room. One day when they were talking, Margaret told Simon about the ghost, and how she always thought of it as a little girl. He realised that, although he had never seen anything or consciously formulated the thought, he had been feeling the same. For him, the awareness of her presence only comes in the evenings, when he has been alone, and neither of his nurses has experienced anything of the haunting.

Just off the waiting room and reception area is a little room with original Tudor beams, which was apparently built as a play-room for the first owner's children – he had nine of them. On the beams are some paint marks believed to date from that time, done, perhaps, by one of the children. Could it be that the ghost is that of the young artist, who four centuries ago expressed herself on the walls of this little room? Have the manifestations been going on consistently since then, or have they a more recent cause? Whatever the answer, Margaret Stone and Simon Hocken are both convinced that they work in a building with the unseen presence of a lively, high-spirited girl, and are quite happy to share the space with her.

The Museum, 70 Fore Street

One of the most famous buildings in Totnes, this is a nationally important example of a rich Elizabethan merchant's house. Built around 1575, it has seen a great deal of life in its four hundred years and is full of atmosphere, which most visitors find pleasant. No one, local or tourist, should miss a walk around the Museum, and many are surprised to find it is bigger than it looks from the main street.

Before it was bought by the then Borough Council in 1958 and put to its present use, the house was owned by a Mr Kinsman, who ran it as a tea shop. He told a local doctor that it had two ghosts, a man and a woman, but unfortunately I have not been able find anyone who can tell me any more about them. Bill Bennett, the curator for eight years until his retirement in October 1992, who is, amongst many other things, another ex-mayor of Totnes, says he has never felt anything in the building except friendliness, and he has been alone in it "all hours of the day and night." The previous curator has also told me that she never saw or heard of any haunting. Nevertheless, some people do feel there is 'something' around, and shortly before the close of the 1992 season a teenaged boy came downstairs in 'a very shocked condition' after seeing a ghostly figure in the reconstructed Victorian grocer's shop, a place where another person also says she is aware of a 'presence.' So, although you will probably enjoy every minute you spend in the museum, it is just possible you will see or feel something out of the ordinary.

The little path on the left-hand side of the Museum building, leading to the courtyard, garden, Study Centre and to Manor Cottage, also, for some, has a strange atmosphere. Personally I have always found it very attractive, leading up between old walls with patches of green shining out vividly against the cobbles and the dark stone, but I know of one lady who used to live in the town who hated passing it, and a friend tells me she finds the gateway itself strangely off-putting.

Manor Cottage

Next to the Museum along this very pathway, Manor Cottage is a beautifully restored house dating from 1570, with a long garden going back to Victoria Street, one of the original 'burbage plots' of Totnes stretching from the main street to the town defences. Both house and garden are lovingly cared for by the present owners, who have never had any ghostly experiences here. The previous owner, however, encountered a ghost in his sitting room one night. A major feature of the cottage is a large old fireplace and oven, and he was sitting by it when suddenly the room went very cold, and he saw the figure of a woman bending over the oven, as if working at it.

King William IV Hotel, Fore Street

This red-brick building with a pleasing curve as it meets the main street is a rarity, an inn that can be precisely dated. Above the entrance are the two dates 1830 and 1902, referring to the first pub on this site, built in the year William IV ascended the throne, and the present one, which was rebuilt at the turn of the century.

Known to the locals as the 'King Bill' it has always been a basic, unpretentious town pub and commercial hotel, which in early years doubled as a bus depot. In the mid 1970s it was taken over by Jackie and Ron Hodder, a cheerful, no-nonsense Cockney couple, who kept it until 1988, since when it has been refurbished in the usual style of the '90s.

A feature in the *Totnes Times* for February 26th 1981 told of how Ron and Jackie had grown used to the ghostly activities of an entity they called 'Bill', who played around with the lights, jammed doors, moved things about and on one occasion pulled somebody out of bed!

Both of them had a strong sense of 'Bill's' presence. He was believed to have been a former cook at the hotel, who died in one of the upstairs rooms. In 1979 some visitors staying at the pub actually met and talked with the ghost. They found, in an attic room, an old man who complained about the noise of music coming up from the bar. This old man turned out to be 'Bill.' Many people, regulars at the pub at that time, will testify to the ghost's existence, but he appears to have ceased his haunting, as the current landlord, when I asked him about ghosts, was quite emphatic that there aren't any there now. So it seems that the only spirits you will find at the King Bill these days are the ones that come in bottles (if you are writing about pubs and ghosts, you have to get that one in somewhere)!

Lloyds Bank Passage, Fore Street

On the left as you go down the hill from the pub, between the optician and Lloyds Bank, is a little passage containing some offices and business premises. The rooms here were, at the end of the last century, a girls' school known locally as Miss Pinn's School, after one of the founders, and it could be that a schoolmistress of the time still occasionally appears in one of the rooms. Some years ago a ladies hairdresser had her business here, and entering her kitchen one day for a tea break, she clearly saw a lady dressed in the clothes of the last century. A moment later the figure was gone.

The Haunted Newspaper Office, Fore Street

Our local weekly newspaper the *Totnes Times* was founded in 1860 by Theodore Hannaford, but throughout its early years was mainly associated with his nephews, A.E. and T.C. Mortimer, who continued to be closely connected with all aspects of the paper until their deaths in 1909 and 1914. Both brothers were deeply involved in Totnes life, and as well as being journalists and men of affairs they found time to write and publish local guide books; their romantic little book on Berry Pomeroy Castle was the official one for many decades, and can still be found regularly cropping up in second hand bookshops, though alas I have never managed to come across their *Guide to the River Dart*. The brothers lived with and were looked after by their sister Kate, who was devoted to them and their work, and she it is who is believed to have continued to haunt the premises at 34 Fore Street where, for over a century, the *Totnes Times* was written, edited and printed, there being an extensive printing works at the back.

The haunting began a few years after her death, and was accepted as part of life by those who worked on the paper. Her favourite place seemed to be a narrow passage between the offices and the printing works, and her presence was often felt by people walking to and fro. But her main occupation was rearranging and muddling pieces of copy and, in some cases, making them disappear altogether. A journalist who worked for the paper in the 1960s remembers Kate's activities well: "I was working late with a colleague, correcting proofs, when we distinctly heard footsteps in the passage. Knowing that every door was locked I went down the stairs, but found no one. The next morning several pieces of copy were missing. This sort of thing happened on many occasions, and lots of people felt that there was an unseen 'someone' in the building."

Whether or not Kate was always to blame for things that went wrong, she was generally felt to be a friendly ghost who merely wanted to maintain her influence on her family's paper, if only by being a bit of a nuisance!

The *Totnes Times* has moved twice since then, and now is no longer printed in the town at all. The present offices in Warland are free of any ghostly goings-on. The original office at 34 Fore Street is now an Estate Agent's, while the printing works have been replaced by a small housing development called Times Mews. The people who work in the Estate Agency tell me they have never encountered any signs of a ghost, so it seems that with the moving of the newspaper, Kate's reason for haunting has gone, and she has faded away.

Chadder's Penance, Town Marsh

Most of the ghosts in this book have been actually experienced by somebody. In contrast, the traditional ghosts of folklore are hardly ever seen or heard. The stories about them are usually very stylised and predictable, being a strange mixture of pagan, pre-Reformation and later Christian beliefs. Many of them are revenge fantasies about people who were unusually wicked, successful or clever in life, and who pay for it afterwards by being given impossible tasks like making ropes of sand or emptying pools with holed vessels. Probably the best-known Devon story is that of Benjamin Gear or Gayer of Okehampton, who haunts Cranmere Pool on Dartmoor. In her study of such tales, *The Fate of the Dead*, the Devon folklore expert Theo Brown refers to one about a character from Totnes, a French inventor called Chadder. The late Miss Brown gave me the story as she found it in some papers belonging to the Benthall family of Kingsbridge and Totnes, who once had a house on the Plains.

Chadder was related to the Benthalls in some way, and he arrived in Totnes with two friends towards the end of the seventeenth century. He was apparently a very clever man, who benefited the town in a number of ways (unfortunately we are never told what exactly he did) and eventually rose to be mayor, despite the hostility and suspicion of many of the locals. He kept a pet monkey, which did nothing to add dignity to his office. It once broke into an old lady's house, stole a purse of gold coins and distributed them to the children of the town from the mayor's roof. On another occasion it took its master's wig, which was eventually discovered during a banquet – in the pudding! M. Chadder got his come-uppance after his death when he was condemned to the futile task of tying up the River Dart with ropes. At that time there was, it seems, at the end of Town Marsh, a device called the 'buttle hole', which had some kind of valve for preventing the water at high tide from flooding the marsh. The pressure of air and water made a roaring sound, which, the people said, was old Chadder crying for more rope!

Chadder had a son, William, who became a Totnes doctor but who, in his youth, had been well-known as a bird catcher. A Non-conformist Minister once asked a local "Who was Belshazzar?" and the man replied "Bill Chadder? Knawed 'un very well sir. Clever young man, that. Could whistle down a linnet as well as any caal bird!"

What are we to make of this story, which seems to have been totally forgotten in Totnes? The Benthall family papers are vague on dates and details, and the elements of the legend, including the monkey and its tricks, conform to the usual pattern of such tales. A William Chadder was, indeed, mayor of Totnes in 1749 and 1760, but if he was the French inventor who arrived at the end of the previous century, he would have been a very old man by the time of his second term of office. It is more likely that the mayor was his son, the doctor. It no doubt made a better story for the brilliant and eccentric foreigner to have achieved this distinction rather than his son, and made his indignity after death all the more striking. Unfortunately, nothing is recorded of William's two years as mayor.

And what about that wonderfully-named piece of engineering, the 'buttle hole'?

Town Marsh stretched from the end of the Plains to St Peter's Quay, ending at the stream, now covered over, in front of the Steam Packet Inn. It was still marsh at the end of the seventeenth century, as the Town Marsh Gateposts, dated 1687, which stood on the Plains near the converted chapel, can still be seen, rather forlorn and forgotten, next to the Plymouth bus stop. By the end of the eighteenth century the marsh had been reclaimed and planted with trees, becoming a pleasant riverside walk and bowling green. Later it became a busy industrial quay, and now the area is destined for housing development. No one knows exactly when the marsh was drained, but it was probably in the first half of the eighteenth century, when a lot of this kind of improvement was going on, in Totnes and elsewhere. Maybe Chadder the inventor had something to do with this. Perhaps the marvellous 'buttle hole' was his creation? This could easily, in the popular mind, be turned into the story of his voice being heard when it was in action.

Whatever the truth, Chadder has long since ceased his labours, and although at low tide the covered stream still makes a rushing noise as it enters the river, the 'buttle hole' too has vanished into limbo. Perhaps its name should be remembered in the new development on the site?

Steam Packet Inn, St Peter's Quay

This is another friendly local with, it seems, a friendly 'presence.' The Steam Packet, delightfully situated with its beer garden next to the River Dart, is an old building of many different periods, which has been an inn for at least 150 years. Early in 1992 it was purchased by travel writer Simon Cole, who says he was "immediately aware of there being 'something' in the place." Doors would open and shut on their own, lights be played about with and even the water was turned on and off. But Simon is happy with his home, and doesn't feel there is anything unfriendly or unwelcoming about the haunting. "I'd hate it if it was spooky, and would move out tomorrow," he told me. Nor have any of his customers or residents complained about the ghost.

The Spreyton Spectrum

Before we cross over into Bridgetown, here is another traditional tale of how, in the seventeenth century, an old lady from Totnes found herself mixed up with one of the strangest cases of the supernatural of the time, much to her annoyance! This is one of the best known Devon ghost stories and has been retold several times, but is worth including here because of its intrinsic interest and Totnes connection.

The story, which was first reported in a pamphlet published in 1683, begins in the remote village of Spreyton on the northern edge of Dartmoor, between Okehampton and Crediton. It is said that on a clear day, you can, from the top of Spreyton church tower, see the whole of Devon from coast to coast and to the borders of Cornwall, Somerset and Dorset. The village is also meant to be the home of Uncle Tom Cobley and the rest of the ill-fated crew who set out for Widecombe Fair in Devon's most famous song. However that may be, one day in the autumn of 1682, nineteen-year-old Francis Fey was out working in the fields for his employer, Philip Furze. Suddenly there appeared before him the ghost – or 'spectrum' as it says in the pamphlet – of his master's deceased father, whom Francis recognised by a long pole the old man had always carried for killing moles. The ghost explained that several of his legacies had still not been paid, and he wanted Francis to deal with them, as his employer was obviously not bothered about doing so. The young man replied that one of the people mentioned had himself died, and the ghost told him to pay the money to the next of kin. He then instructed the lad to take twenty shillings to his sister, a gentlewoman of Totnes, after which he would not be troubled again. The spectrum went on to roundly abuse his second wife, although Francis, who had known the lady, considered her to have been a 'good woman'.

Francis saw to the spectrum's requests, and finally rode to Totnes with the twenty shillings for the old man's sister, who, however, would have nothing to do with such a dubious gift, claiming it came from the Devil, an understandable reaction at a time when the church frowned on all manifestations of the supernatural. As the youth had come such a long way, however, she allowed him to stay the night at her house, and while he was there the spectrum appeared again. Francis explained that he had done his best, and the ghost had promised to leave him alone. The old man told him not to worry, but to go into town and buy his sister a ring with the money, which she would accept. The next morning Francis did this, and the old lady agreed to take it. Francis rode back to Spreyton, and the spectrum was seen no more.

This wasn't the end of the story, though, for just as he got back to the village another ghost appeared, the wife of the old man who had been so insulting about her! Despite Francis' high opinion of the lady she was obviously upset that he had carried out her husband's wishes, and for many months she plagued him with what we would now recognise as classic poltergeist behaviour. The disturbances were witnessed by many people including the authors of the pamphlet, the local parson and a neighbouring JP. The wife seems to have spent her fury around Easter 1683 and poor Francis was left alone. The old lady in Totnes, if she ever heard any more about it, no doubt gave thanks that she had got off so lightly.

You can learn more about ghostly goings on in Spreyton in *Weird and Wonderful Dartmoor* by Sally and Chips Barber.

Four Seasons Guest House, Bridgetown

More than once during my researches for this book I have come across unexpected material by just casually mentioning what I was doing. In such a way I learnt about the haunting of this guest house in Bridgetown, run by George and Heather Lucas. They also keep the Bridgetown Dairy, right next to it, and when I was in there one day buying cat food, I just happened to ask them if they knew of any local ghosts. "We've got one here," they said, and told me about a shadowy figure that was seen on the stairs a few years ago by two girls who were in the hall. Nothing more is known about this haunting, which has certainly never put anyone off staying with them.

The Old Forge Hotel, Bridgetown

Our next story is unique, being not so much about a ghost as a helpful spiritual presence, apparently that of a devoted craftsman who wanted to help his successor.

If you turn right from the main road in Bridgetown between the two corner shops into Seymour Place, you come to an attractive village-like area where Weston Lane joins Weston Road, full of pretty cottages, old walls and the quiet green of the churchyard. Here you find what is probably the oldest building in Bridgetown, the Old Forge. A focus for the local community for maybe six hundred years, it has been in its time a smithy, a wheelwright's shop, a coach building works and a hay barn. There is even a small lock-up where offenders waited for the magistrate who held court in an upstairs room.

The forge was worked until 1948, and two years later the Duke of Somerset, whose family had owned the property for centuries, sold it off. By 1985 it was very run-down, but in that year Peter and Jeannie Allnutt came upon it and, despite its semi-derelict state, felt immediately drawn to the place. Since then they have completely restored the building and run it as a hotel, while Peter has brought the smithy back to life with a flourishing wrought iron business.

It is only fitting that such a place should be haunted. A medium friend of the Allnutts has, on several occasions, been aware of the welcoming presence of an old lady's ghost in the lounge, and the workman who helped clear out the old prison cell said he felt there was something very strange there, although the reality is that nothing so dreadful could have happened in it – nobody languished there for very long. But the main presence at the forge, less a ghost than a guiding spirit, has been an entity called 'Harry' whom Peter believes was the last blacksmith to work there.

The first indication that someone might be there was when some of the early guests kept hearing unmistakable 'blacksmith' type sounds coming from the smithy at night, and they would say to Jeannie that they couldn't understand how her husband had the energy to work all night after spending the day on the building. The answer was that he didn't work all night! The Allnutts never heard the sounds, only their guests. 'Harry' really began to make himself felt when Peter's first customer at the smithy, a local titled lady, brought him a ceremonial sword, its handle full of jewels, which needed repairing. Not sure how to do the job without melting the jewels, he put it on one side and got on with something else. Then one morning he came down knowing exactly what to do, and felt that the information had been given to him by another person – 'Harry'. He is very clear about the feeling that the knowledge came from someone else; it was not that he had just given his mind time to work things out. After this he felt Harry's presence regularly, guiding his hands and showing him how to do things. This continued until April 1991. Peter feels that his helpful guide has now moved on to another life and has left him to work on his own, trusting his beloved forge to his successor.

Coldharbour Cottages, Bridgetown Hill

The main road towards Paignton and Torquay climbs steeply up Bridgetown Hill. On the right, just above the Cottage Hospital, is Coldharbour, a pleasant row of 19th century stone cottages with leaded windows and a cosy, old-fashioned feel to them. Coldharbour is an old name, usually found on the outskirts of a town beside an ancient highway, which perfectly suits this site, as this was the main road to the far west, crossing the Dart at a ford, long before Bridgetown or Totnes came into existence. As it suggests, the name indicated a place of refuge for the traveller, particularly for soldiers, but only of a spartan and basic kind – rather like an old-style youth hostel. Students of the ley-line system believe it also to denote the presence of their mysterious energies.

Happily the cottages today belie their name, but a friend who lives in one of them tells me that she often hears very loud footsteps running around, as well as bangs and other noises that could not originate in the house or either side of it, or even from the road. Although the walls are thick and sounds from neighbouring cottages do not usually penetrate, she has also heard, quite clearly, the chiming of a non-existent clock in the night.

Weston House

Right at the very top of Bridgetown, actually in the parish of Berry Pomeroy, is Weston House. This rambling mansion was built during the nineteenth century, apparently by a former Duke of Somerset for one of his lady friends. The story I have been told is that she was interfering too much with his life in London, so he gave her this home deep in the South Devon countryside, where his family still own a good deal of property, to keep her out of the way! Let us hope she appreciated the great beauty and peacefulness of her surroundings. The house is now divided into many different flats and dwellings. One of the people who lives here tells me that he has often heard, at night, footsteps that, he is sure, cannot be caused by any of his neighbours. The layout of the house has changed so much that the sounds cannot possibly be coming from where he hears them, unless they are echoes from the past.

Windwhistle Cottage

High above the River Dart, a mile or so downstream from Totnes, opposite the salt-marshes at World's End, is the atmospheric ruin of Windwhistle Cottage. Visible for miles in many directions, it stands out dramatically and draws attention to itself. Although just the broken-down shell of a house, little more today than a façade, it exerts a fascination, up on its hill, that compels many people to make the climb for the sake of the views and the romantic appeal of being at a ruin. Those who are less able or inclined to exert themselves to that extent can still enjoy it by taking a boat trip down the Dart; from the river the view of the place, two hundred feet up, is unforgettable.

Windwhistle was originally a farm-labourer's cottage belonging to Lower Weston Farm, Bridgetown, and is still the property of the farm; strictly speaking, there is no public right to go there without permission. It was last inhabited at the turn of the century by a family called Steer. Mr Steer, as could be expected of someone living in such a definite statement of a house, was a bit of a character. He had 19 children, kept as many pigs and sheep, and practised as a 'quack vet.' I have been told that the cottage in those days was whitewashed and had a tiled roof. Now, however, it is just a few old walls and feels very remote, with only the cries of the sheep, the mewing of buzzards and the never-ending sighs of the wind.

Such a place just has to be haunted! I am not aware that anyone has actually seen or experienced anything other than the atmosphere of the place, but the story was told in Berry Pomeroy a few years ago that the cottage was the home of the Duke of Somerset's last gamekeeper, who murdered his wife there. One of them – I'm not sure who – continues to haunt it. It doesn't really matter; the place itself is a ghost story!

Bowden House

Bowden House, situated about a mile out of Totnes on the Ashprington road, has in recent years become one of the most successful tourist attractions in the area. Its history goes back to 1154 when it was owned by the De Broase family, who rebuilt Totnes Castle, and later it was owned by the Black Canons of Canonsleigh.

In the sixteenth century it became the property of the Giles family, said to be the richest people in the county, and at this time a Tudor brick mansion was built here. Later it belonged to the Trists, who in 1704 gave the house its Queen Anne façade that visitors enjoy today.

Bowden is now owned by the Petersen family, who have restored it and made it an imaginative, worthwhile place to visit, with guided tours around the house and a unique collection of cameras in the British Photographic Museum. You can learn more about Bowden's history in *The Great Little Totnes Book* by Chips Barber and Bill Bennett, but what concerns us here are its hauntings.

A place with such a rich, colourful past is bound to have a few ghosts, but actually there are so many it is difficult to know where to start! Cats, dogs, monks, children, Elizabethans and Regency Dandies have all been apprehended here. People have reached out and had their hand taken by unseen entities. There is a very common feeling, experienced by family, friends and visitors, of being watched. The Petersens' maintenance man for many years had so many psychic inspirations and warnings that he came to accept them as a fact of life.

Monks, presumably Black Canons, have often been seen, and their chanting is frequently heard in the main house and the courtyards. A visitor from New Zealand was once staying in one of the cottages, and woke up one night to see a monk leaning over the bottom of his bed, peering directly at him. The monk wore a black habit with a knotted cord round the waist, and his cowl emitted a darkish blue light, but there were no discernible features. The man watched the monk for a full ten minutes. Another monk has been seen in the nursery of the main house, this time wearing a brown habit, walking slowly about the room. His cowl shone with so bright a light that the whole large room was illuminated.

On many occasions the Petersens have been showing visitors around the house, and things have been seen, heard and felt by people who had no idea, until that moment, that it was haunted. In the library a figure has sometimes been glimpsed through a crack in the door leading to what was, in the eighteenth century, a powder closet. When the door is opened, the figure vanishes. During a tour in 1986 a middle-aged lady started to shake in fear and repeatedly shouted, "It's coming towards me, what am I going to do?" No one else saw or felt anything frightening. On another day, the guide entered a room full of visitors who were waiting for him, and saw a woman brushing angrily at her skirt and saying, "Get down dog, who let this dog in?" She was the only person to see the dog.

One day the Petersens noticed a visitor walking around the house holding a branch from a beech tree. When they asked why she was doing this, she replied that it was, "To ward off evil spirits in the house."

On August Bank Holiday 1988 people in several groups saw the ghost of a little girl in a long blue dress. One lady, walking down the stairs from the gallery, was heard to say, "I must hold on to the bannister." She crossed from the centre of the stairs to the bannister, and said later it was because she had seen a little girl with long auburn hair and a blue dress standing on the stairs. The lady had actually walked round the girl. Another woman came to Mrs Petersen on the same day to ask if the house was haunted, as she had seen the girl sitting in a chair in the Pink Room. These sightings seemed to confirm something said by a clairvoyant who had visited the house the year before, and claimed to pick up the spirit of a little girl of the pre-Victorian period (presumably he meant the early nineteenth century) who had died in the Pink Room. She had not been a member of the family, but had been much loved. The girl was also seen during the 1950s, when Bowden was used as a children's home. One of the 'old girls' returned for a visit and saw the child at an upstairs window.

Mr Petersen's most unnerving experience occurred when he was working with some medieval stone, dug up in the grounds. Suddenly he saw the whole of his arm and hand outlined with light. It was several days before he could bring himself to tell his wife what had happened.

Lest I put you off going there, I hasten to point out that most visitors to Bowden thoroughly enjoy the experience, and even of those who pick up something strange, the majority find it startling but not terrifying! It just appears that, for some reason, Bowden is one of those places where the energy of past ages is somehow accessible. Hauntings continue, so this is definitely a place to be psychically on your toes.

Dartington Hall

Dartington is a large, straggling village a mile or so north west of Totnes. There is no real centre, but rather a series of quite separate little settlements, with a main focus for the community at Shinners Bridge, where the A384 from Buckfastleigh meets the A385 from Plymouth. The other important focal point at Dartington is of course the vicinity of the Hall, high up above a bend in the River Dart.

Dartington Hall is generally agreed to be the most impressive medieval manor house in Devon, on a scale much grander than any other. It was built by John Holland, Duke of Exeter and half-brother to Richard II, in the fourteenth century. From the sixteenth to the twentieth centuries, the Hall was the home of the Champernownes, at first one of Devon's leading families, though as time went on their importance became more exclusively local. By 1925 the Great Hall was in ruins and the estate in very poor shape, but in that year it was bought by Dorothy and Leonard Elmhirst who, with a great deal of vision, idealism and the money to put it into practice, made Dartington the centre for a bewilderingly wide-ranging experiment in the revitalisation of rural life, involving education, the arts, business, building, agriculture, forestry and crafts. Many of the social, economic and educational ideas developed at Dartington have had far-reaching effects. The balance between ideals and commerce has never been easy, and Dartington today is made up of very different elements from those of the '20s and '30s – the famous Progressive School has gone – but 'Dartington Hall', in its muddled diversity, continues to enrich, stimulate, entertain and infuriate the area as it has for nearly seventy years.

For over three centuries the estate was the home of one family and naturally, with the generations living and dying at the rambling Hall and its environs, a number of traditional ghost stories came to be told. All the ghosts were very conventional – a phantom coach with a headless horseman that was said to go through the lodge gates at the end of the drive; a White Lady who glided along the road to the Hall; a Grey Lady seen in the vicinity of the old church tower who possibly haunted the spot because she had thrown herself from it; various shades and apparitions in the house and garden. By the twentieth century most of this was nearly forgotten. Dartington under the Elmhirsts was rationalistic, liberal and progressive, and though it is now veering towards a fashionable concern with the ecological and holistic, there was little room for such things as ghosts in its decidedly humanistic philosophy.

Nevertheless, sensitive people over the years have had psychic experiences at Dartington, and even some of the traditional spectres have been met with. In the 1920s a young postman from Totnes and a servant girl from the Hall encountered the White Lady on the drive, and the poor man never recovered from the shock, dying soon afterwards of a brain fever. The coach and horses have not been seen within living memory, but some people feel uncomfortable at the end of the drive where it used to appear. The Grey Lady is well known, or at least well talked about, in the area of the Great Hall, and drivers on their way home from plays and concerts have swerved to avoid a shadowy figure who may or may not be she. Many people feel that the gardens are haunted. One lady has told me of how, walking through them one summer evening in 1977, she suddenly found herself stepping into the past. It was as if she was momentarily taken over by, or walked into the body of, someone else, and she felt the rustling folds of an old-fashioned dress about her. She stepped out of the experience as suddenly as she had stepped into it.

It has often been reported that ghostly music has been heard in parts of the Hall area. Some people who experienced this several years ago remember the occasion clearly. Peter Kiddle, then a tutor at Dartington College of Arts, his wife Cathy and a friend, were sitting having a drink in the White Hart bar after a concert. The bar at that time was a lot smaller than now, and people would overflow into the dining room, actually the medieval kitchen. Closing time came and went, and they found they were the last people in the building. It was approaching midnight and they decided they ought to go, when all three heard music coming from the Solar, a long narrow room reached by some stairs in the dining room. It sounded like a piano or harpsichord, and they wondered who could be playing so late at night. They crept up the stairs, quietly so as not to disturb the player, but found the door locked. There is another door into the Solar at its far end, up some spiral stairs near the entrance to the Great Hall. They went to this other door and, still hearing the music, pushed it open. The piano was at the end of the room near the first door, the locked one. There was no light in the room, but they could all see, in the moonlight, a man, whom nobody recognised, sitting playing the piano. He wore evening dress and had dark hair and a ruddy complexion. The three walked slowly into the room and the man, apparently annoyed at being disturbed, got up from the piano and went towards the locked door. They followed him down the room but he had vanished, although there had been no time in which to unlock the door. They hurried back the way they had come, into the dining room and up the stairs; the door was still locked, and there was no sign of the man. They decided it was time to go home!

A few days later they examined the Solar and found, near the piano, the outline on the dark panelling of what had obviously once been another door, though it was not in a place where there could ever have been one. They discovered later that the panelling was not original to Dartington, but had come from an old manor house in Yorkshire at the time when the Elmhirsts were rebuilding. Did the ghostly musician come all the way with it? Peter Kiddle remembers telling Leonard Elmhirst, who died in 1974, about their experience, and how he just nodded and said, "Yes, I know."

Over at the other end of the Great Hall, in what was once the Elmhirsts' private house, music has often been reported being heard in some of the rooms.

Some Haunted Lanes

All my life I have walked through the green lanes in every direction around Totnes, and have often felt that many have a haunted quality about them, even if it is only a sense of continuity with the past rather than the actual presence of a ghost. Winding between high Devon hedgebanks, dense with ferns and hogweed, nettles, docks and brambles, rich in the spring with primroses, bluebells and campions, often almost impassable and more like water-courses in the winter, they have an appeal that never fails. And there are certain places along them that seem haunted in a more precise way. On Sharpham Drive, for instance, where it gets to the gate at the top and changes from being a lane to a field path, I am not alone in noticing a strange atmosphere, and somebody has told me that, many years ago, she saw here the figure of a man dressed in early nineteenth century costume. Another lane that has a peculiar ambience is Harper's Hill, known locally as the 'Roman Road.' A Roman road it is not, but it is nearly as old, being part of the ancient highway to the South West centuries before Totnes was established, and it is easy to feel, walking up it, so close to the town but suddenly so remote, that you are in a place where ordinary life is suspended.

The lane that many local people say has a real sense of being haunted is Bourton Road, off Bridgetown Hill, which leads into a network of narrow lanes going to Littlehempston, Gatcombe and Berry Pomeroy. There is no doubt that a lot of people recognise and respond to a haunted, haunting quality about the whole vicinity of Berry Pomeroy, centred of course on the castle but pervading a wider area. Someone who lived in the village once told me it was like being suddenly engulfed by a cloud as soon as she reached the edge of the affected area. This lane seems to definitely lie within the influence of the 'cloud.' One lady, who has walked here regularly for years, tells me that at a certain spot, where there is a gate on the right into a field with a little spinney in it, she invariably experiences a great feeling of sadness and oppression, as does her husband when he is with her. She senses that this negativity is related to Berry Pomeroy Castle which, indeed, is not far off across the fields, though hidden by dense woodland.

She feels strongly that there is a connection here with one of the legends associated with the castle, that of the unfortunate lovers. There was once a feud between the Pomeroys and another local family (it is not known which one). A Pomeroy daughter fell in love with the son of the rival house, but they had to meet secretly to avoid parental disapproval. One day the girl's brother discovered them and, to save, as he saw it, the family honour, promptly stabbed them both to death. One account of the castle's hauntings says that the lovers can be seen reaching out longingly to each other across an impassable barrier, but this sounds more like romantic invention than a genuine ghost story. Although the incident is meant to have taken place right next to the castle, my informant is certain that her feelings here are related to the tradition in some way.

Another lane near Berry Pomeroy, and maybe within reach of its strange spell is the deep pack-horse lane running from above Weston, at the top of Bridgetown, down to Fleet Mill. In my book on the River Dart I referred to this lane being reputedly haunted by the ghost of a young woman, though no story is attached to her. Certainly it is a lane with a mysterious, remote beauty to it, so that, walking along hidden by trees and ferns, with the immense hillsides rising up all round, it would not be at all surprising to find oneself encountering this gentle figure from another time.

The story of the haunted castle and all the ghosts associated with it, most of which are a lot more frightening than any to be found in Totnes, is told in Deryck Seymour's *The Ghosts of Berry Pomeroy Castle.*

Earth Mysteries Around Totnes

Perhaps the simplest kind of haunting is the one that we can all relate to: the overriding atmosphere of a place. There are houses which, for no obvious reason, are always depressing or always cheerful, some that feel as if they have known nothing but tragedy and gloom, others that seem to have been (or, in Totnes, probably have been) blessed and dedicated to the growth and healing of everyone who visits them.

The same is true of other places, woods, fields, hills, certain spots along roads and, as we have seen, old lanes. That there are particular places, certain forms in the landscape, that are especially inspiring, awesome or even sacred, is another common experience. This brings us to that range of subjects now known as Earth Mysteries – ley-lines, landscape energies, terrestrial zodiacs, sometimes even UFOs. About these things I am open-minded, in fact I am willing to be convinced, but somehow I have never seen quite enough evidence to push me into wholehearted belief. I have no problem with the idea that the earth itself is a living entity; the concept is ancient and universal, and has acquired scientific respectability recently as the 'Gaia Hypothesis.' I can even see the logic in the theory that there are pressure points and energy flows on the earth's surface like acupuncture points on the body. In my years of walking around Totnes and its surrounding countryside I have always felt that there is a deep harmoniousness, a basic 'rightness' about the setting of the town. The commonsense view is that this is because I am at home here, but maybe it is not too great a step to wonder if there is not some subtle force actually in the landscape, that was recognised and manipulated in early times to bring out the best in it.

Real or not, ley-lines are said to radiate outwards in every direction from Totnes, and pass through its major buildings. It has also been put forward that the whole area of the

River Dart can be interpreted as a Landscape Temple. Its 'head' is in the upper reaches above Buckfastleigh, its 'heart' between there and Totnes, centring on Dartington, and the estuary from Totnes to Dartmouth corresponds to the lower part of the body. Residence in, or attunement to, a particular part of the Temple stimulates the appropriate qualities and functions. I have not heard that anyone has yet found a zodiac in the countryside around Totnes, like the ones at Glastonbury and elsewhere, but it would not surprise me in the least if someone did.

Whatever you think of all this, at least such beliefs lead to a respectful, less aggressive approach to the earth and the life upon it which can only be good. And the experience of something either sacred, powerful, disquieting or even alien in certain places cannot be denied, even in the gentle environment around Totnes. Someone more sensitive to this than I am writes:

There are places – very often those associated with hauntings or strange manifestations – where I feel that my surroundings 'shift'. A slight alteration in the passage of time, a shrug as though Man and his meagre machinations are held in contempt by the landscape. In one place, I actually felt that it was I who was doing the haunting, in a freakish departure from the human concept of time. I think it is not a matter of 'wild versus tame' but more basic than either of these ideas; complete spaces where even change needs no indication or scale.

With such intriguing speculations and questions we will finish this ghostly ramble around historic Totnes. I have no doubt that there are stories I have missed, so if you have ever seen or experienced anything in the way of a haunting, or know of any queer tales about places in the town, please get in touch.